Poland

Dunajec

Bardejov

Kežmarok

Spisska
Kapitula

Poprad

Presǒv

Levoca

Košice

Ukraine

Hungary

N

E

S

0 — 200 m = 0 - 656 ft
200 - 500 m = 656 - 1640 ft
500 - 1000 m = 1640 - 3281 ft
1000 - 1500 m = 3281 - 4921 ft
1500 - 2000 m = 4921 - 6562 ft

0   25 km

0   25 miles

Looking at Europe

Slovakia

Dr Daniel Kollár

The Oliver Press, Inc.
Minneapolis

This edition published in 2006 by The Oliver Press, Inc.
Charlotte Square
5707 West 36th Street
Minneapolis, MN 55416-2510
USA

Published by arrangement with KIT Publishers, The Netherlands, and
The Evans Publishing Group, London, UK, 2005

Library of Congress Cataloging-in-Publication Data

Kollár, Daniel.
    Slovakia / Daniel Kollár.
        p. cm. -- (Looking at Europe)
    Includes index.
    Contents: History -- The country -- Towns and cities -- People and culture -- Education
-- Cuisine -- Transportation -- The economy -- Tourism -- Nature.
    ISBN 1-881508-49-8
    1. Slovakia--Juvenile literature. I. Title. II. Series.

    DB2711.K65 2006
    943.73--dc22

                                                              2006040088

Text: Daniel Kollár
Photographs: Jan Willem Bultje
Translation: Howard Turner
US editing: Holly Day
Design and Layout: Grafisch Ontwerpbureau Agaatsz BNO, Meppel, The Netherlands
Cover: Icon Productions, Minneapolis, USA
Cartography: Armand Haye, Amsterdam, The Netherlands
Production: T & P Far East Productions, Soest, The Netherlands

Picture Credits
Photographs: p. 6, 8, 10, 11 (c), 11, 13(b),15 (b), 16 (c, b), 18 (t), 19 (b), 23 (r), 24 (t), 39 (t), 40 (t),
42 (b), 44 (t), 4 (t): Ján Lacika; p.20, 42 (t), 44 (b): Maria Zarnayova; p.37 (t): Samuel Kubani;
p.37 (b): Peter Hudec; p. 46 (b): Milan Kosec: EPA Photo, CTK; p. 19(t) © Shepard
Sherbell/CORBIS SABA; p. 19(b) © Liba Taylor/CORBIS; 23(b) © Wolfgang Kaehler/CORBIS;
25(b) © Reuters/CORBIS

ISBN 1-881508-49-8
Printed in Singapore
10 09 08 07 06   8 7 6 5 4 3 2 1

Contents

Introduction

Slovakia is located right in the heart of Europe. It was once part of the Hungarian Empire and later the Austrian Habsburg Empire. Over the centuries, its borders have changed dramatically. Until quite recently, it was part of Czechoslovakia, and it only became an independent nation in 1993.

Slovakia lies between Poland in the north and Hungary in the south. To the west it is bordered by the Czech Republic and Austria, and to the east lies the Ukraine. The border with the Ukraine is the shortest, at only 60 miles in length. Slovakia is completely landlocked. The nearest sea is the Adriatic in the south (224 miles away). The Baltic Sea lies some 273 miles to the north. Although the area has been subject to invasion and occupation over the centuries, Slovakia now maintains good relations with all its neighboring countries. Trade links are improving, and transport to and from cities in Slovakia to other European destinations – notably Vienna in Austria and Budapest in Hungary – is efficient and easy to use.

The Slovak people are descended from the Slavs, who migrated to the region in the early centuries AD. Many tribes settled in the areas that are now Slovakia and the Czech Republic during this time and, eventually, they were united into one kingdom. For centuries, it was effectively ruled by the kings of Hungary,

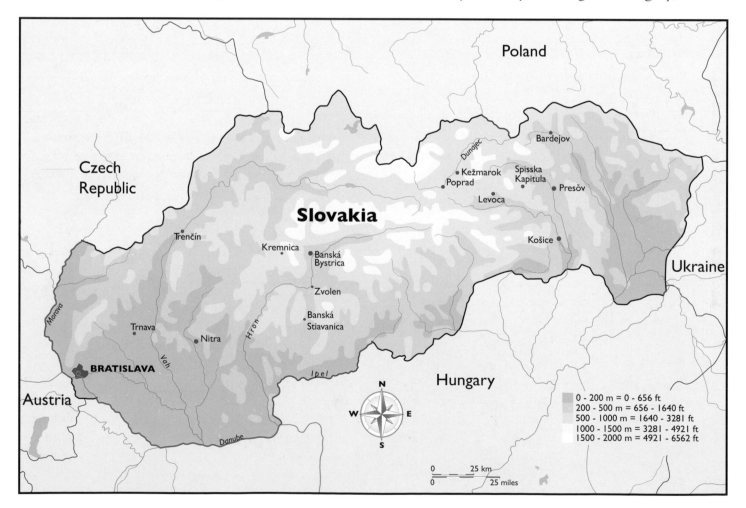

▶ *The top of Mount Lomnicky is one of the highest peaks in the Tatra Mountains, which lie on the border between Slovakia and Poland. A cable car runs to the top of the mountain.*

eventually evolving into the Habsburg Empire – one of the greatest and longest-lasting empires in European history. Since 1993, however, the Slovak people have had their own country, and their customs and traditions have endured through this long period of being ruled by – and being part of – other countries. Slovakia's government is now a parliamentary democracy, with a national council, a president as head of state, and a prime minister as head of government. In 1995, a law made Slovak the only official language of the country, although Hungarian remains widely spoken.

Slovakia is known for its natural mineral and thermal springs. Spa towns have grown up around these, attracting people from Slovakia and other European countries, who come to bathe in the therapeutic waters.

One of the most important features of the Slovakian landscape is the Tatra mountain range, which is part of the Carpathian Mountains in the north of the country. These not only provide some of the most dramatic of the country's landscapes, but are also home to many species of flora and fauna, and some of the finest forests in Europe.

All these features are attracting increasing numbers of people to Slovakia, and although it is not yet a major industry, tourism is starting to contribute more to the economy. The economy has also been assisted by improved international and trade relations, enhanced by Slovakia's membership in international organizations, such as the European Union, which it joined in May 2004.

◀ *This spot by St. John's Church in Kremnické Bane in Slovakia is believed to be the geographical center of Europe. However, both Lithuania and Poland also claim to be home to the middle of Europe.*

History

The territory of Slovakia has been settled since ancient times. More than 100,000 years ago, Neanderthal people lived next to the hot springs below the Tatra Mountains. The first farmers, who built simple dwellings and lived in communes, arrived around 5,000 years ago.

▼ *The castle in Trenčín is one of the largest in Slovakia. On the rock on which the castle stands is an inscription celebrating the Roman victory over the Germanic tribes.*

The Celts settled in the territory in the fourth century AD. They built fortified settlements, smelted iron, and struck coins. They created the first civilized society to settle in the region, and were followed by Germanic tribes and Romans who crossed the River Danube. These two peoples fought each other on Slovakian territory in AD 179 – a campaign the Romans won. This victory is commemorated by an inscription dating from this ancient time on the castle rock in the town of Trenčín.

The Slavs

The first Slavs arrived in the region between the River Danube and the Tatra Mountains at the same time as many other migrating peoples. They lived in tribes, built small houses, and worked the fields. They were forced to defend themselves against their more powerful neighbors and, to do this, all the different Slav tribes united. In the seventh century AD, they were led by the Frankish merchant Samo, who had founded the powerful Samo's Realm – the first western Slav state.

By the ninth century, Samo's Realm had disappeared, and the Slavs had founded the even more powerful Great Moravian Empire. This was, in fact, the first common state comprising Czechs and Slovaks (decendants of the Slavs). This was also the time when the missionaries Constantinus and Methodius from the Greek town of Thessaloníki were invited to Moravia in order to spread the word of Christianity and gain converts. The brothers produced the first writings and promoted religious services in local languages. The greatest ruler of the empire was Svätopluk (AD 871–894). During his rule, the Great Moravian Empire thrived and became an important European power.

▲ *This statue of the Greek missionaries Constantinus and Methodius can be found in Nitra, in western Slovakia.*

The three rods of King Svätopluk

When this powerful ruler was dying, he summoned his three sons, Mojmír, Svätopluk, and Predslav. He gave a rod to each of them and asked them to break them. The young princes easily broke their rods. Then the king tied the three rods together and asked his sons to break them again. This was a rather more difficult task to accomplish. "As you see, my sons," said the old king, "if you hold together, nobody will defeat you. But if you do not, you will be doomed to failure." However, the sons did not listen to their father's advice, and after his death they quarrelled and fought between themselves. This resulted in the decline and the eventual disintegration of the empire.

Hungarian rule

After the fall of the Great Moravian Empire at the beginning of the tenth century, Hungarian tribes conquered the territory of Slovakia. The region became part of the kingdom of Hungary for a period of 1,000 years.

The first king of Hungary was Stephen I, from the Arpad dynasty. He was crowned by the pope on Christmas Day in the year 1000. Stephen I was later declared a saint because, as a ruler, he adopted the Christian religion and founded churches and monasteries all over the kingdom of Hungary.

In the thirteenth century, the Tartars (tribes from central Asia) attacked and plundered the entire kingdom of Hungary. After their retreat, the Hungarian rulers started building stone castles to defend themselves against further attacks and the king, Belo IV, invited colonists from Germany to resettle the deserted and ruined territory.

The new German settlers and the Hungarians worked together to rebuild the country. Eventually, the area became very prosperous. Mining towns such as Banská Štiavnica, Banská Bystrica, and Kremnica, where gold, silver, and copper ores were extracted, generated considerable wealth. The centers of commerce at that time were the towns of Bratislava, Trnava, Košice, Levoča, and Bardejov. During the reign of the wise and powerful King Matthias Corvinus, the first university, the Academia Istropolitana, was founded in 1467.

Habsburg rule

In the early sixteenth century, the Turks attacked Slovakia and other areas, including present-day Hungary. Many regions fell under Turkish rule, but Slovakia managed to stop the Turks from gaining the upper hand, and so it became the center of the Hungarian Empire. The capital was moved to Bratislava (then called Pressburg). By this time, the king of Austria, Ferdinand I, had also claimed the Hungarian throne, making Hungary really a part of the Austrian Habsburg Empire.

The Habsburgs tried for many years to drive the Turks out of this region of central Europe, and for the next 200 years, many battles were waged on Slovakian lands. By the time the Turks were finally defeated, the country was once more in a state of ruin. Many people lived in abject poverty and there was a big divide between rich and poor.

▲ The small mining town of Bratislava became the Hungarian capital in the sixteenth century. The castle can be seen on the left.

Robbery became a way of life for many people, who could not afford to live any other way. A famous Slovakian folk hero emerged at this time – a Robin Hood figure called Juraj Jánošík, who took money and jewels from the rich and gave them to the poor.

During his short life (he died at the age of 25), Jánošík became the greatest Slovakian legend for the common people. Tales of his

◀ Bratislava Castle, where many kings and queens were crowned, still stands today.

exploits were told to children and written down in books and songs. He is still a great Slovakian folk hero today.

The economic situation in Slovakia only began to improve in the eighteenth century, when Empress Maria Theresa made many important changes to the law, including tax reform. She also made education compulsory, ordering that every child must attend school (she had 16 children herself!). Her laws helped to bring prosperity to the country.

The road to independence

In the nineteenth century, the Slovaks began to assert their national identity. They established a literary language and drew up a political program. However, like all the other "nations" included in the Austro-Hungarian Empire – Serbia, Croatia, Romania, and others – Slovakia was still not considered a nation in its own right. This only happened when the empire dissolved at the end of the First World War, in 1918. The Slovak nation joined the Czech nation to form a common state called Czechoslovakia.

In 1939, the German leader Adolf Hitler ordered that Czechoslovakia should be split up, and the Slovak people found themselves part of an independent country led by President Joseph Tiso. Although the people protested, Tiso let German troops into Slovakia, and the country sided with Germany in the Second World War. After the war, Tiso paid dearly for this decision. He was tried and executed as a Nazi collaborator, traitor, and war criminal.

Czechoslovakia was restored after the end of the Second World War. It was ruled by the Communist Party of the Soviet Union from 1948 until November 1989, when the communist regime collapsed. This set Slovakia on the path to democracy.

The death of Juraj Jánošík

Jánošík was captured, tried, and sentenced to be hung from his left rib. As he stood at the gallows, he was allowed to express three wishes. His torturers permitted him to say goodbye to his beloved sweetheart, to dance his favorite dance, and to smoke a pipe. They would not release him from his chains, though, so Jánošík had to dance with them round his ankles. He was a strong man, and he danced nine times around the gallows, then finally he jumped up and hung himself on the hook. He then asked for his pipe. Jánošík hung there on the hook, smoking his pipe, for three whole days. By the time he had finished his last pipe, the emperor's messenger had arrived with a pardon for him. But Jánošík was already more dead than alive. His last words were: "As you have baked me, you will also have to eat me!"

▲ Habsburg Empress Maria Theresa

The joint state of Czechs and Slovaks was dissolved once again, and an independent Slovak Republic was declared on January 1, 1993. Slovakia is now a sovereign independent country, with its own president and democratic elections. The country is a member of NATO, and it joined the European Union on May 1, 2004.

◀ Maria Theresa in a coach on her way to Bratislava Castle

The country

▲ *At more than 8,700 feet, Gerlachovský štít is Slovakia's highest mountain.*

Slovakia is a landlocked nation in the middle of Europe. In fact, it claims to contain the geographical center of Europe – in the vicinity of St. John's Church in Kremnické Bane, a village in central Slovakia. Slovakia covers about 18,800 square miles and has around 5.4 million people.

The northern and northeastern frontiers of Slovakia run along the Tatra range of the Carpathian Mountains, and this forms a natural boundary between Slovakia and Poland. The southern and southwestern frontiers – the boundaries with Hungary and Austria – are marked by three rivers: the Morava, the Danube, and the Ipel. Slovakia is referred to in many traditional poems and songs as the "country lying between the Tatra Mountains and the Danube River."

Mountains

The peaks of the Tatras are more than 8,000 feet high. The tallest were formed by glaciers many centuries ago. This area includes some of the most dramatic landscapes in Slovakia, with glacial valleys, mountain lakes, and waterfalls. The Carpathian Mountains consist of several ranges, which are separated from one another by depressions, or basins, arranged in a line and often connected by valleys. This alternation between mountain ranges and lowland areas is typical of Slovakia's geography.

▼ *The jagged peaks of the Tatra Mountains*

Kriváň – symbol of Slovakia

Like the Greeks, the Slovaks have their "Mount Olympus" – Mount Kriváň, located in the Tatra Mountains. Although it is not listed among the 25 tallest peaks in Slovakia (it is only 8,182 feet high), its strange formation has inspired poets, writers, painters, and artists. Gold-miners, botanists, travelers, and even kings have visited it. Its name refers to its crooked top ("krivý" means crooked in Slovak). It is the subject of many folk legends. One of them tells how, on the seventh day of creation, God ordered one of the angels to scatter the last sackful of His creation all over the world. But when the angel flew over the Tatras, he struck one of the peaks with his wing and the sack split open. Lakes, waterfalls, and many animals fell to Earth. The top of the peak was bent over and this is how Mount Kriváň was formed.

▲ *The Danube flows past the capital, Bratislava.*

▶ *High mountains make way for rolling hills.*

Some of Slovakia's most famous features are its limestone caves, many of them in the mountain regions. Several of these are open to the public, and it is possible to explore the chambers. Many of the Slovakian caves are included on the UNESCO list of World Cultural and Natural Heritage.

Lowlands

Slovakia has three main lowland areas: the Záhorská nížina lowland in the west, the Východoslovenská lowland in the southeast and the Podunajská nížina lowland in the southwest.

Rivers and lakes

The Danube is the largest river in Slovakia. It flows from Germany and Austria, and also forms the boundary between Slovakia and Hungary. Its water level is highest in summer when glaciers melt in the Austrian Alps. Other Slovakian rivers, such as the Váh, Hron, and Ipel are high in March. The longest Slovakian river, the Váh, flows almost the whole length of the country.

The majority of lakes in Slovakia were formed by glaciers. Almost all of them are located in the Tatras. Each lake has a different color, which is determined by its surroundings and composition. Glaciers have also carved out waterfalls in the Tatras. The highest of them (its individual steps are about 260 feet high), the Kmet'ov vodopády Waterfall, is tucked away in the remote valley of Nefcerka.

Springs

Slovakia boasts a great number of mineral springs and huge reserves of groundwater. Springs are scattered all over the country, while the groundwater reserves are concentrated around the River Danube in the south. Many of Slovakia's mineral springs are believed to have health-giving properties and, for centuries, people have visited them for healing purposes.

There are more than 1,200 mineral springs in Slovakia, and hardly a region of the country is without one. There are also many hot (thermal) springs, with temperatures of over 68°F, in Slovakia. In many places, spa towns have grown up around the mineral and thermal springs. The spa of Piešťany in western Slovakia is world famous. Its springs have temperatures in excess of 140°F. Other spas include Trenčianske Teplice, Bojnice, and Sliač in central Slovakia, and Bardejov in the northeast.

▲ Many guests come to the resort at Bardejov to enjoy the thermal springs. The sign (left) explains that Napoleon's second wife, the daughter of Emperor Franz (Francis) I of Austria, Empress Marie Louise, visited the resort in 1809.

"Once a week we go to the springs to fill our bottles and jugs with water from the spring," Peter says. "We turn the event into a day trip and the whole family comes along: my father and mother, my brothers and sisters as well." His father is filling a bottle. It takes a while, because there is only a trickle of water. Later, they will have a picnic in the park, where they will drink the wholesome spring water out of the bottle and eat the bread and sausages they have brought along.

Climate

Slovakia's climate is moderate, although the weather is different in the lowlands and in the mountains. The lowlands are dry and warm, and the weather is usually predictable. In comparison, the mountains can be more cool and more humid, and the weather is more unpredictable. The warmest place in the country is the Podunajská nížina lowland; the coldest are the Tatra Mountains.

The coldest and warmest months of the year are January and July, respectively. Tropical days, when the daily temperature exceeds 86°F, and tropical nights when the temperature does not drop below 68°F, are frequent in summer. In winter, the temperature often drops below zero, and in the mountain valleys it can fall to -4°F.

▲ Springtime in the foothills of the Tatra Mountains brings a blast of color in the flowering meadows.

The driest part of the country is the Podunajská nížina lowland, where the total annual rainfall is between 20 and 24 inches. The Tatras form the most humid area and the precipitation – in the form of both rain and snow – amounts to more than 80 inches a year. There is continuous snow cover from November to May, and it has even been known to snow in the summer. The most rainfall occurs in June and July, and the least occurs in the autumn months.

The individual seasons of the year are clearly discernible in Slovakia, and each of them has its own special charm. Spring is remarkable for the flowering meadows. Summer is characterized by maturing fields and children bathing in the lakes. Indian summers – periods of constant sunny weather – are typical of autumn in Slovakia.

Winter in Slovakia is fairly harsh, especially in the north, where the snow cover lasts more than 100 days (200 days in the Tatras). Although it is very cold, this weather does offer the opportunity for skiing or sledding. The winter landscapes in Slovakia can be very dramatic.

◄ Winter in Slovakia can be cold – temperatures regularly drop below freezing. In the background is Mount Kriváň.

Towns and cities

The first towns were established in Slovakia in the eleventh century, and there are now 138 towns and cities across the country. The largest of these are Bratislava and Košice. Today, the majority of the Slovak population – 60 percent – lives in a town or city.

▼ *Hlavné námestie is the main square in Slovakia's capital, Bratislava.*

HLAVNÉ
NÁMESTIE

▼ *The Old Town Hall sits in St. Martin's Square, and is one of the oldest stone buildings in Bratislava – built in the fourteenth century.*

Bratislava

Bratislava is the capital of Slovakia and the largest city in the country, with around 450,000 inhabitants. It extends along both banks of the River Danube in the extreme southwestern part of the country, a short distance from both the Austrian and Hungarian borders.

People settled in this area in around 4000 BC, when the Celtic and Germanic tribes first came to Slovakia, and its location on the river and at the heart of Europe has meant that people have settled here continuously since that time. It became the capital of the Hungarian Empire in the sixteenth century.

Today, Bratislava is a thriving modern metropolis and the main tourist destination in Slovakia. It is not only an important commercial and industrial center, but is also the heart of Slovakia's cultural and artistic life. Most of the important academic and administrative institutions can be found in Bratislava, including the main universities, foreign embassies, and government buildings.

The city is dominated by the castle and St. Martin's Cathedral, which is located in the heart of the old town. The cathedral was built in the fifteenth century. It was here that the rulers of the former kingdom of Hungary were crowned for nearly 300 years.

The castle was the seat of the Hungarian kings, and has been the most important feature of Bratislava since the fifteenth century. It was destroyed by a fire in 1811, and was not fully reconstructed until the middle of the twentieth century.

▲ *Bratislava grew in importance in the sixteenth century, when attacks by the Turks in surrounding areas forced the Hungarian rulers to move the capital here. It is now a bustling city on the banks of the River Danube.*

▲ *A statue of St. George defeating the dragon, in the courtyard of the Archbishop's Palace in Bratislava*

▶ *Narrow medieval lanes crisscross the old town in Bratislava. Most of them open on to the main square, the Hlavné námestie, which has the Maximilian Fountain at its center.*

Nitra

Nitra is another very old town, located in western Slovakia. It was once the seat of the rulers of the Great Moravian Empire. The dominant feature of the town is Nitra Castle, which dates from the eleventh century. Not far from Nitra is the town of Trnava, which is known as the "Rome of Slovakia" because it has so many churches.

Banská Bystrica, Kremnica and Banská Štiavnica

Banská Bystrica, Kremnica, and Banská Štiavnica are all former mining towns located in central Slovakia. Copper was once mined at Banská Bystrica, Kremnica was famous for its mint (coining), and Banská Štiavnica was a center for silver mining – one of the most important mining towns in Europe. The first European university to offer training for people who wanted to become mining experts was opened in Banská Štiavnica in the eighteenth century. The town's main attraction is the open-air mining museum, where visitors can explore one of its now-inactive mines. Banská Štiavnica was registered on the UNESCO list of World Cultural and Natural Heritage in 1991. Kremnica has been producing coins since the fourteenth century, and still does so today.

▲ *St. Nicholas Church is one of the oldest in Trnava. Construction on it began in 1380.*

Levoča and Kežmarok

Levoča and Kežmarok lie in the area known as Spiš, in the shadow of the Tatra Mountains. This was the region of Slovakia that was settled by German colonists in the thirteenth century. Levoča is famous for its many stately homes, the sixteenth-century town hall, and St. James's Church, which is a place of pilgrimage.

▼ *This stately home in Levoča has been turned into a movie theater.*

▲ *The square in Kremnica. The town's attractions include the mint, a castle, and a number of museums.*

Another attraction is the Mariánska Hora basilica and shrine on the hill above Levoča. Every year in July, thousands of Catholics gather here to venerate the Virgin Mary.

Levoča's twin town is the neighboring Kežmarok, which has landmarks such as a wooden church dating from the early eighteenth century, and the fifteenth-century castle.

▶ *Many newlyweds choose the fountain in Košice as a romantic setting for their wedding photographs.*

▼ *St. Egidius Church and the town hall in Bardejov are just two of the town's many Gothic buildings.*

Košice

Košice is a metropolis in eastern Slovakia. It is the country's second-largest city, with around 242,000 inhabitants. Its most important historic building is the Cathedral of St. Elisabeth, which dates from the fourteenth century, and is the largest Gothic church in Slovakia. Locals often pass the time of day on Sunday afternoons in the central square.

Bardejov

Bardejov lies in northeast Slovakia. This is a famous spa town (see page 12), but it also has a number of other attractions. In fact, it boasts more Gothic monuments than anywhere else in the country. These include St. Egidius Church, dating from the fifteenth century, and the Gothic-Renaissance town hall, with its precious collection of religious icons. The town walls of Bardejov are the best-preserved medieval fortifications in Slovakia.

People and culture

Slovakia has about 5.4 million inhabitants, with an average of 228 people per square mile. However, this population is not evenly distributed throughout the country. The basins and lowlands are densely populated, while fewer people live in the mountainous regions.

Villagers normally live in detached houses, but in the cities, a large number of people live on housing estates, such as the Petržalka quarter in Bratislava, which has almost 125,000 inhabitants.

Maria and Jan are having their wedding photos taken in Košice. "This is the biggest day of our lives!" Maria says with a radiant smile.

There are several marriage traditions in Slovakia. One of them is the breaking of a plate at the reception. The bride and groom clean it up together as a sign of them working as a team in the future. The number of pieces of the broken plate that they miss represents the number of children they will have.

At midnight, all the guests form a circle around the couple. A hat is passed round and people "buy" a dance with the bride or groom. The money is a gift to the couple to help them start their lives together.

Population

The largest section of the population (86 percent) is Slovak. The largest minority group in Slovakia is the Hungarians, who make up 10 percent of the population and who mostly live around the southern border of the country. A substantial number of Roma (Gypsies) also live in Slovakia. They are estimated at around 400,000, although no one knows their exact numbers, as many of them claim either Slovak or Hungarian nationality. The Roma mostly reside in the eastern and southern parts of Slovakia.

Czech and Ukrainian minorities also live in Slovakia. Slovakian legislation guarantees that the languages of these minorities will be used in towns and villages where they make up more than 20 percent of the total population. One visible effect of this regulation is the road signs, which appear in Slovak and in the language of the minority in those particular areas.

Emigration

At several points in its history, a large proportion of the Slovak population has emigrated to other countries. These occurrences are referred to as "emigration waves," and there have been different reasons for this at different times.

In the nineteenth and early twentieth centuries, many Slovaks abandoned their homeland and went to settle in the United States. The reasons were largely economic – times were hard in Slovakia. The second emigration wave, which followed the end of the Second World War, was motivated more by political reasons and the search for a more tolerant and freer environment than the reigning communist regime allowed.

Today, more than two million Slovaks live outside of Slovakia, the majority of them in the USA. One of the most famous people to originate from Slovakia, but find success in another country, was Andy Warhol – a famous artist who pioneered the style known as "Pop Art." Warhol's parents came from eastern Slovakia.

▲ *These Slovaks are of Roma, or Gypsy, descent. Roma people have settled all over Central Europe, but in many places they still suffer discrimination, which can lead to unemployment and poverty.*

Language

The official language of the country is Slovak, which is strongly related to Polish and Czech. The language is written in the traditional Latin alphabet, to which diacritic marks (accents) have been added. Vowels with an accent – á, é, í, ó, ú and ý – are long vowels and are pronounced in a more drawn-out way than those without an accent.

◄ *New houses are being built right on the edge of farmland.*

◄ This church in Smolnik was built in the eighteenth century. In those days, the town was famous for its copper and silver mines.

◄ A religious procession taking place near Levoča

Religion

The majority of Slovaks are religious people. Slovakia is usually considered to be a Catholic country, as Catholics make up as much as 69 percent of the total population. The second most-represented religion is the Evangelical Movement. Greek Catholics, or members of the Orthodox Church, live in the eastern part of the country. About 15 percent of the population does not belong to any Church or religion.

▼ The view from the castle in Trenčín. Across the rooftops, you can see St. Francis Xavier Cathedral (the square tower on the left) and the monastery (the yellow building on the right).

▲ *The church in Spišská Kapitula*

Churches

The first churches were built in Slovakia in the ninth century, during the period of the Great Moravian Empire. None of these old buildings have survived, though. The oldest church that still exists in Slovakia is located in Kostol'any pod Tribečom, in western Slovakia. This dates from the first half of the eleventh century. Two wonderful cathedrals were constructed in the Gothic period (from the twelfth to the fifteenth centuries) – St. Martin's Cathedral in Bratislava and the Cathedral of St. Elisabeth in Košice.

There are many wooden churches in Slovakia. Several of these were built during the reign of Emperor Leopold I in the late seventeenth century, during the time of the Reformation. The emperor granted the Protestants the right to build some Evangelical churches in certain parts of the kingdom. However, he said that they must be located outside the nearby settlements, were not allowed to feature a tower, and their entrances had to be pointing away from the settlement. Moreover, the builders were not allowed to use stone or iron. This is why most of them were built of timber, without the use of even a single iron nail. The high points of folk architecture in Slovakia are the wooden churches in the north-east of the country, which demonstrate the skill of the old traditional craftsmen. They date mostly from the eighteenth century, and many of them contain precious icons.

St. James's Church in Levoča is probably the most frequently visited church in Slovakia. Visitors come to see the late-Gothic main altar of St. James, which is the highest altar of its kind in the world (60.5 feet). It is made of lime-tree wood and its creator, Master Pavol of Levoča, carved it at the beginning of the sixteenth century. The altar has statues of the Madonna with Child, St. James and St. John. They are extraordinary pieces of art.

▼ *Wooden churches like this were constructed by traditional craftsmen and builders, and can be found in the north and east of the country.*

◄ *The logo of the most popular television station, Markíza*

Media

Slovakia has a number of television channels and radio stations. The most popular television channel is the privately owned Markíza Channel. Czech television channels can also be received in Slovakia. The most-listened-to radio stations are OKEY and Fun Radio. They play contemporary music around the clock and are especially popular among younger members of the population. Modern telecommunications have also become increasingly common in Slovakia in recent years, and nearly four million people have mobile phones.

▼ *On a nice day, groups of musicians can be seen performing in the street.*

More children than ever are computer literate. In the larger cities, almost every family owns a personal computer and has access to the Internet. Internet cafés, which can now be found in most towns and cities, are favorite meeting places for young people. The number of people owning mobile phones is also on the increase.

Slovaks, especially the young, love to visit nightclubs in towns and villages on weekends. Going to the movies is also a favorite pastime. Most modern movie theaters can be found in the city centers. They usually show American films, which are the most popular among young Slovaks.

Festivals

Several festivals and commemorative days are observed in Slovakia throughout the year. The first celebration of the year is on January 1 – the Day of Foundation of the Slovak Republic. On January 6, Epiphany (or the Day of Kings) is celebrated to commemorate the day the three wise men reached Bethlehem. Orthodox Christians also celebrate Christmas on the same day as elsewhere.

February and March make up the liveliest season of the year, called *Fašiangy* in Slovak. This is a period of fun to celebrate the coming of spring. Many dances are held, and it is the most popular time of year for weddings. It lasts until Ash Wednesday – the first day of Lent.

Summer is the season of musical concerts and folk festivals, which are especially popular in Slovakia. On November 17, Slovaks commemorate the anniversary of the "Velvet Revolution" and the fall of the communist regime on what is called the "Day of Fight Against Totality."

▶ *Fašiangy, the Slovakian carnival, with song, dance and people in costumes*

The end of the year is marked by preparations for Christmas. St. Nicolas's Day on December 6 is a festival especially loved by children because it is when St. Nicolas, accompanied by the "devil" dressed in a black fur coat, visits children. St. Nicolas brings the good children fruit and sweets, while the devil "frightens" children who have been naughty. On December 13, St. Lucia's Day, groups of women traditionally visit men and try to "frighten" them. The end of the year culminates with Christmas trees and special family gatherings.

Health care

Health care is available for everyone in hospitals or clinics in all Slovakian towns. Larger villages also have their own health-care centers. In case of serious injuries or sudden illnesses, immediate medical assistance is available via the emergency telephone number 155. There is also a confidential telephone line available for both adults and children who wish to discuss any health or psychological problems.

Government

Slovakia is a parliamentary democracy with a president who is elected every five years. The president shares power with the parliament. The official name of the parliament is the National Council of the Slovak Republic, and it has 150 members. The deputies in the Council are elected for four years. The most important Slovakian document is the Constitution of the Slovak Republic, which was drawn up in 1992. The government of the Slovak Republic is led by the prime minister. The president, parliament, and government run the country from the capital, Bratislava.

◀ *The parliament building in the Slovak capital, Bratislava*

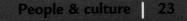

Shopping

The shops and the range of goods sold in them are very similar to those in the rest of Europe, especially the shops and food markets in the towns and cities. Many supermarkets are open around the clock and offer a wide variety of products. Shops are also open throughout the night – summer and winter – in almost all the larger villages and in the main tourist centers. Although the smaller villages may not have the variety of products to be found in the towns, basic foods and commodities are available even in the smallest and most remote communities.

▲ ▶ Fresh and home-grown produce is available daily at markets across Slovakia.

Markets are very common in Slovakia, and almost all towns and villages have one. They sell fresh fruit, vegetables, poultry, flowers, and other produce. Not all markets are outdoors. Many towns have covered markets, too. In Bratislava, there is a large indoor market. Locals go there to do their shopping and to enjoy traditional Slovakian food, such as wine, sour cabbage, or freshly baked bread. At Christmas, a special market is held in Bratislava's main square, where there are many stalls and lively festive music.

People visiting Slovakia who want to buy traditional Slovakian goods that are not available in other countries can purchase items made by local artists and craftsmen. These handicrafts include dolls in national dress, embroidery, pictures painted on glass, or wood-carved pieces of art. Among the most popular souvenirs are the traditional Slovakian musical instrument – a decorated flute – and models of the historic weapon of legendary Slovakian outlaws – an axe.

▼ Megastores like this are usually built on the outskirts of the towns and cities, where there is enough space for parking.

> "When the Slovakian ice hockey team played in the finals of the World Championship, the streets were deserted as everybody was at home watching TV," Kamila tells us. "We were sitting at home with our friends and watching the match. When Peter Bondra scored the winning goal, we started celebrating, and after the game had finished everybody went out into the streets, which were jam-packed with cars. People were honking their car horns and everybody was laughing, singing, and shouting with joy."

Sport

Slovak children usually support their local athletes. Soccer is the most popular sport in Slovakia, and the people follow their local and international teams avidly.

In recent years, however, it is the ice hockey team that has brought Slovakia attention in the international arena. In 2002, they beat Russia to become world champions. Tennis is also a popular sport, and the famous tennis player Martina Hingis was born in Slovakia.

◀ Slovak hockey player Peter Bondra celebrates a goal during the 2002 World Championships. Bondra has played in more than 1,000 NHL games.

Education

The current education system in Slovakia is loosely based on the one established by Empress Maria Theresa in the eighteenth century. However, in the following century, many Slovakian schools were closed and children were forced to study in Hungarian, a language foreign to most of them.

In 1948, after the Second World War and the establishment of the communist regime in Slovakia, all schools came under state control and the education curriculum focused on the teachings of communism. When the regime finally collapsed, churches and private schools were re-opened and institutes of higher education, including universities, were set up.

Primary education

Children in Slovakia can attend nursery schools from the age of three. Here they play and get used to being around other children. Compulsory education begins at the age of five and, when they are six, children start primary school. Compulsory education lasts for ten years in Slovakia.

▲▼ *Slovak children make their way to a secondary school, or gymnasium. Classes start at 8 o'clock in the morning.*

Gabriel and his classmates are telling us about their school. "We are students at the city secondary school," explains Gabriel. At the age of ten, children can choose between staying on at primary school for a second level, lasting a further five years, or going to a secondary school, like Gabriel. There are also highly selective academic schools called gymnasiums. Most children who gain a place at a gymnasium go on to attend universities, but competition to get into these schools is high, and only around 12 percent of students who apply get in.

One of the most important subjects learnt even at primary schools is a foreign language. Children can choose between languages such as German and English, and some schools also teach French, Italian, or Spanish.

Secondary education

After five years at the first level of primary school, children have a choice about their further education. They can stay on for a further five years at the second level of primary education, or they can go on to secondary schools. These include grammar schools, where they learn several different academic subjects, or vocational schools, where the teaching is more specialized and focused on practical subjects. There are also special schools for gifted children. Here, they can choose from a variety of artistic or sports-oriented schools. However, these special schools also have classes in basic subjects like the Slovak language, math, and foreign languages.

▲ *Slovakian story books, like this, are used in primary schools.*

► *These young boys are playing outside their school during the long break in the morning.*

Subjects that are believed to require the most attention, such as languages and math, usually make up the first two or three lessons of the day. The third lesson is followed by a long break, during which pupils normally hang around chatting in the school corridors or in the playground. Lunchtime is normally between noon and 1 pm. Lessons for older children continue after lunch. Younger children can attend the after-school club, where they play or do their homework for the next day.

Although the official language for teaching is Slovak, minorities living in Slovakia have schools of their own, in which all lessons are held in their own language. There are many Hungarian and Ukrainian schools in Slovakia.

At the end of secondary school, all students take school-leaving exams. If they pass these, they are eligible to apply for a place in the university or one of the technical institutes in Slovakia to continue their education.

Higher education

At present, the most celebrated university in Slovakia is the Comenius University in Bratislava. However, there are many other places students can go for higher education. The Slovak Technical University, also in Bratislava, is popular with students interested in technology. The Institute of Economics is also becoming increasingly popular. Some students prefer to study abroad. Before admitting students from Slovakia, some foreign universities require a certificate stating that they had previously been accepted at one of the national universities.

The general level of education in Slovakia is reasonably high. Over 85 percent of the population has completed secondary school, around 41 percent of the working population has received higher vocational training, and 12 percent has attended a university.

◄ *Comenius University in Bratislava — one of the most prestigious universities in Slovakia*

"I don't live here," explains Anja. "I'm staying in Bratislava with my cousin." She and her cousin are having a game of soccer in the peaceful courtyard of the Archbishop's Palace in Bratislava. "I'm from Germany," she says. "We have a mid-term break during which I usually come to Slovakia. Both my parents work, so at home I would be alone all day and I'd get very bored!"

Time off

In the evenings and during the school vacations, there are plenty of activities to keep children busy. Most young people enjoy sports and the majority of them play soccer or ice hockey. However, in recent years, the rise in the number of home computers has resulted in fewer children taking part in outdoor activities, and many of them now enjoy playing computer games or watching television in the evenings. They also have homework to do for the next day. Some children take part in extra-curricular activities such as art or dance lessons. Others learn to play a musical instrument after school.

On weekends, children often travel with their parents to weekend cottages. This is especially true of children who live in the towns, for whom it offers a good opportunity to experience nature and life in the countryside.

▲ *In the evenings and on weekends, many children enjoy their leisure time at open-air pools like this one.*

School vacations

There are different sorts of holidays throughout the year, including days off for particular celebrations such as Slovak National Uprising Day. The winter vacation lasts for two or three weeks. There is nearly always snow on the ground at this time of year and children spend a lot of their free time skiing or skating. Spring vacation starts towards the end of February and ends at the beginning of March. This is the best time for spring ski trips.

The Easter holidays only last a few days, but it is a time of great tradition in Slovakia. On Easter Monday, boys approach girls in their family or female schoolmates to "whip" them with the Easter whip and to sprinkle them with perfume or plain water. This is an ancient custom in Slovakia, but the girls think that it's a little unfair! The summer vacation is the longest, and children in Slovakia make the most of their free time in the same way as children all over the world. Summer means swimming, camping, games, hiking, and many other outdoor activities.

Cuisine

Slovakia has several traditional dishes, and most restaurants will have these on the menu so tourists can try genuine Slovakian cuisine. Soup is particularly popular in Slovakia, and the favorite meat is pork. Because the country is landlocked, there is not much fresh fish available, although the Slovaks do have fish farms, which breed fish such as carp and trout.

In Slovakia, lunch is usually served between 11 am and 1 pm. It usually consists of two courses – soup and a main course (either meat or fish). People have dinner in the evenings when everyone in the family has come home from school or work, usually between 5 pm and 7 pm.

Recipe for bryndzové halušky

Ingredients

2 or 3 potatoes
1 egg
4 to 5 tbsp flour
Salt

Feta cheese
Bacon pieces
Cream cheese

Peel the potatoes and dice them finely or slice them very thinly. Add the egg, flour, and a teaspoon of salt and mix it all into a dough, then knead well. Bring a saucepan of salted water to boil. Take a scoop of dough with a tablespoon and let it slide into the boiling water. Do this with the remainder of the dough. Make sure the water stays boiling. When the balls float to the surface, they are done and you can scoop them out with a skimmer. Keep them warm.

Fry the bacon pieces in a pan, then add the feta and the cream cheese, and allow them to melt. Put the warm balls in a dish and pour the bacon and cheese sauce over them.

Bryndzové halušky

This dish is to the Slovaks what pizza is to the Italians or sushi is to the Japanese. It is dumplings made from potatoes, mixed with a special kind of sheep cheese called *bryndza*. Fried bacon is laid on top of the dumplings before serving. Slovaks usually have skimmed or sour milk to accompany bryndzové halušky. The dish is so popular that a competition is held every year in the village of Turecká to see who can make the most delicious bryndzové halušky.

Other traditional meals are prepared with potatoes, cheese, and cabbage. A good Slovakian lunch must contain some kind of soup, prepared with beans, beef or chicken, or sour cabbage. Pork and chicken are popular, and carp is a favorite fish among Slovaks. One of the most popular dishes is a stew made of pork, called szegedinsky gulas. This is stewed pork, sauerkraut (pickled cabbage), spices, and sour cream. Pork is also often served in a spicy potato pancake.

Slovakia's most popular dessert is pancakes. These are usually served filled with jam, ice cream, and chocolate sauce, raisins or nuts, and whipped cream.

School meals

Children in Slovakia love milk and milk products. For breakfast, they often drink a cup of tea or cocoa, which is accompanied by some bread or a pastry. In the morning, parents often prepare sandwiches and a piece of fruit for their children to take with them to school. They eat this during the mid-morning break.

Some schools provide what is known as a "milk breakfast" – a glass of milk served during the break. Lunch is normally provided at school and it consists of several dishes, starting with soup, followed by a main dish of meat and potatoes or rice, and ending with fruit or cake.

Eating out

The opening-up of Slovakia to the rest of Europe has resulted in, among other things, the importation of foreign dishes, such as pizza from Italy. Fast food has also proved very popular among Slovak children. Adults tend to complain that American "take-out" food is slowly replacing the local traditional cuisine.

The range of meals in restaurants is becoming increasingly varied. Traditional Slovakian or central European meals are served in most of them, although international cuisine is also featured on the menus of many restaurants, particularly those in the towns and cities. The number of Chinese, Indian, and Italian restaurants in Slovakia is also on the rise.

◀ *Young people watch a street entertainer making fun of fast-food restaurants.*

Transportation

Slovakia has an intricate road network consisting of highways, first- and second-class major roads, and subsidiary roads. The highway network, which is presently around 155 miles long, is constantly being expanded. A continuous highway between the capital, Bratislava, and Košice is near to completion. In addition to Prague or Budapest, Bratislava will then be directly connected via highway with Vienna in Austria.

▲ *A road winds through the mountain foothills.*

▼ *A new road bridge has been built over the River Danube near Bratislava.*

Railways

Slovakia can be reached by airplane, bus, car, and by boat via the River Danube. Although trains in Slovakia are rather old-fashioned, they are still an important part of the country's transportation system. The railway network in Slovakia, with a total track length of 2,200 miles, connects all Slovakian cities and the majority of villages. The main northern railway track, which leads from Bratislava to Žilina and from there to the Tatras and Košice, is the most important national railway link. International trains mostly use the track running from the Czech Republic to Bratislava and to Hungary.

Tourists from more remote countries normally fly to Vienna in Austria, which is only 37 miles away from Bratislava, and from there, Slovakia is only a bus or train journey away.

▼ *The larger cities have trams like this one in Košice.*

The Vysoké Tatra mountains have a special means of transportation in the form of the "funicular" railway. This is made up of cable-cars, chairlifts, and trams, which travel between the individual leisure resorts in the mountain range. The funicular connecting Tatranská Lomnica and the top of the Lomnický štít peak (the second-highest mountain in Slovakia) rises to an altitude of more than a half mile, and its track is 2.5 miles long.

Buses

Slovakia has one of the best-developed bus networks in Europe. Buses carry passengers to and from practically every town and village in Slovakia. Most of them start in Bratislava, Nitra, or Košice. Normally, people pay the driver when they board the bus, but passengers can also buy tickets in advance at bus stations in larger towns. This is recommended in the case of international journeys, where seating is often sold out several days before departure. As well as traveling to destinations within Slovakia, buses also carry visitors to Bratislava from many European cities, such as Paris, Munich, Stockholm, Brussels, and Prague.

▲ *Buses are one of the best ways to travel to and around Slovakia. There are bus networks connecting most towns and villages in the country.*

▼ *A shunting-yard, where railway carriages are connected to a different engine, moved from one track to another, or held when not in use*

▶ *Taking a boat is a fun way to travel to and from Slovakia. It is possible to take a ferry to major European cities outside Slovakia, such as Budapest in Hungary or Vienna in Austria.*

Shipping

An attractive way of traveling to Slovakia is by boat. The port in Bratislava has regular boat connections with Vienna and Budapest. This mode of transportation is particularly popular with children, who love the boat-trips on the Danube to destinations such as Devín Castle, located near Bratislava, or the picturesque town of Hainburg in Austria.

Aviation

There are a number of international airports in Slovakia, located in Bratislava, Košice, Piest'any, Sliač, and Poprad. Slovakia has several airline companies. The largest of these are the Slovenské Aerolínie and SKY Europe. However, the majority of international tourists use the Vienna-Schwechat Airport, which is only a 30-mile bus ride away from Bratislava.

▼ *Compared with major European airports, those in Slovakia are quite small.*

The economy

Slovakia's closest relations are with the neighboring Czech Republic. Although the nations split in 1993, and each of the countries now has its own administration and economy, their common history, culture, and traditions still hold them together.

The languages of the two countries are very similar, and Czech books and journals are sold in Slovakia. The proximity of the Czech Republic also means Czech radio and television programs are available to Slovaks. However, Czech people generally do not read Slovakian newspapers or watch Slovakian television, and so future generations of Czechs may find it difficult to communicate with or understand people from the country with which they were once joined.

▼ *Industry is an important part of Slovakia's economy. Industrial areas like this can be found in many places across the country.*

Slovakia also has good relations with its other neighboring states. It is a member of what is referred to as the "Visegrad Four" (V4) – together with Poland, Hungary, and the Czech Republic – which was formed to promote closer co-operation in Central Europe. Slovakia has a particularly special relationship with Austria, because it represents the gateway to Europe for Slovakia. The short distance between the capitals of both countries – Bratislava and Vienna – makes it easy to exchange goods and services.

Industry

Slovakia underwent enormous industrialization after the Second World War (when it was still part of Czechoslovakia). The emphasis at this time was on heavy industry – making products such as machinery. However, when the two countries divided and the communist regime collapsed, many companies closed down, and Slovakia suffered widespread unemployment.

Today, Slovakia is an important producer of iron and steel, and of products made of these metals. The gigantic American metallurgical company U.S. Steel purchased the Slovakian company Vychodoslovenské Železiarne in Košice, and this has created many jobs. There are also chemical-industry plants in Bratislava. Two of the most important are Slovnaft and Istrochem, a petro-chemical company. These plants produce several sorts of gasoline, crude oil, synthetic substances, synthetic fibers, and organic-chemical products.

Slovakian textile and cotton manufacturers were among the greatest in Central Europe in the nineteenth century, and this tradition continues today. Slovakian cheeses (bryndza and Liptov), beer (Topvar, Corgoň or Zlaty bažant), and chocolate (Figaro) are among the best in Europe.

Slovakia has a large car-manufacturing industry, mainly because the German company Volkswagen purchased the Slovak Bratislavské Automobilové Závody in 1989, and built a huge plant in Bratislava. A second large investment was in Trnava, where another big plant is under construction, which will produce Peugeot-Citroën cars.

▼ Slovnaft is a plant processing crude oil, located in Bratislava. The company also owns a chain of gas stations.

Slovakia is one of the largest producers of motor vehicles in Europe. This is the Volkswagen plant in the capital, Bratislava.

Agriculture

Agriculture was the main economic activity in Slovakia until the 1950s. Although fewer people make their living by farming today, this industry is still very important. The main type of agriculture is cereal growing. Wheat is grown in the fertile lowlands of the western and southern parts of the country, in the Podunajská nížina lowland. Barley, rye, and oats are also grown in Slovakia – oat-flakes have recently become very popular as a breakfast cereal.

Corn, beets, and potatoes are also important crops. Slovakia offers excellent conditions for growing fruits and vegetables, especially in the south, where there are large orchards with peach, apricot, apple, and cherry trees. Tomatoes, cucumbers, red and green peppers, lettuce, cabbage, celery, and cauliflowers, which are sold in markets all over Slovakia, are grown in the Podunajská nížina lowland.

A harvester in operation, gathering wheat, which is made into cereals

◀ *Tokai wine maturing in oak barrels. It is well-known abroad and is produced in eastern Slovakia.*

Viticulture – grape-growing – is another important branch of agriculture. Cultivating vines and producing wine is one of the oldest Slovakian traditions, and has become a way of life for the locals. An area comprising several villages in the Tatra Mountains is one of the best-known wine-producing regions in Slovakia. The "Wine Path" is designed for tourists and wine enthusiasts, and connects several famous vine-growing localities. Wine festivals are held here every year.

Cattle breeding and fish farming

In the fertile lowlands there are large farms where beef and dairy cattle, pigs, and poultry are kept. The mountain areas of Slovakia are used for sheep farming. In addition to sheep's milk and meat, milk products such as several sorts of cheese, or *bryndza,* are made in this region.

Another important branch of agriculture in Slovakia is fish farming. Large numbers of carp, and other fish species such as trout, are farmed in man-made ponds. These are much in demand, particularly at Christmas, when fish is a traditional dish.

Import and export

Cars and car accessories not manufactured in Slovakia are imported from Germany. Raw materials such as coal, crude oil, and iron ore are imported from Russia. Computers, medicines, and cars are brought in from the Czech Republic.

Until the end of the 1980s, exports from Slovakia consisted mainly of raw materials such as copper, timber, and iron. However, since then, the share of exported finished (value-added) articles has increased. Above all, Slovakia has become an important exporter of motor vehicles to Germany. Despite this, the export of semi-finished articles (iron and steel products, mineral oils, and lubricants) to western European countries still predominates. Slovakia's most important foreign trade partner is the Czech Republic, closely followed by Germany and Russia.

Currency

The official currency of the Slovak Republic is the Slovak koruna (SKK). One koruna is made up of 100 haliers. Coins are available in values of 50 haliers and 1, 2, 5 and 10 koruna (crowns). Banknotes are available in values of 20, 50, 100, 200, 1,000 and 5,000 koruna. One U.S. dollar is equal to about 33 Slovak koruna.

Slovakia in the European Union

The Slovakian economy has slowly improved in the last few years. The ultimate aims are to change and improve the way in which products are made, and to attract foreign interest and trade. The government is also trying to reduce unemployment, which currently exceeds 25 percent in some regions of Slovakia.

The nation's entry into the European Union in 2004 brought numerous challenges for Slovakia. With help from other European countries, Slovakian industries with the most promising outlooks are those related to car manufacturing and materials production. These include glass-manufacturing and shoe-manufacturing, as well as electrical engineering, paper production, and wood-processing.

Slovakia also has great tourism potential, which is not being exploited at the moment. In order to properly take advantage of the travel and tourism industry, Slovakia needs to build more modern and better roads, including highways, and a high-speed rail network.

▼ *The presidential palace in Bratislava, where the Slovak government has made plans for improving the country's economy since it joined the European Union in 2004.*

Tourism

Tourism is not yet a major industry in Slovakia and does not contribute much to the economy. However, more people are starting to come to Slovakia to enjoy the many historical sites and to experience the traditions and customs of the Slovak people.

▼ *The water in this pool is muddy because it comes straight from one of Slovakia's many springs. The water is very fresh and healthy.*

Slovakia is a country in which both summer and winter sports can be enjoyed. The hills at the foot of the Tatra Mountains are crisscrossed by well-maintained hiking trails, cycle paths, and cross-country ski tracks. Water-sports enthusiasts can make use of the rivers and lakes – the Dunajec and Hron rivers are the most popular. Children in particular love the dog-sleigh competitions that are held every winter in Donovaly in central Slovakia.

Lakes and water reservoirs are the best places to visit during the hot summers. However, many Slovak children prefer to go to the outdoor thermal swimming pools, which can mainly be found in the south of Slovakia.

The huge water reservoir of Gabčíkovo on the River Danube is now a favorite place for both national and international vacationers. An excellent water-slalom canal has been constructed next to the reservoir, which is ideal for enjoying rafting or canoeing.

▶ *These children are enjoying a day out on a river raft. Although the country is landlocked, there are many water-based activities in which to take part in Slovakia.*

In many ways, Slovakia is a paradise for tourists, especially when it comes to hiking and cycling. The Vysoké Tatra Mountains, with their many high mountain trails, are the most attractive setting for hikers. The paths take tourists along several routes, where the views include glacial valleys, mountain torrents, waterfalls, and lakes.

As Slovakia is primarily a mountainous country, it is ideal for skiing. The world-famous ski resort of Štrbské Pleso is located in the Vysoké Tatra Mountains, and has ski jumps, cross-country, and downhill ski slopes. There are many other ski resorts in Slovakia where international winter sportsmen and women practice, including Jasná in the Nízke Tatra Mountains and Vrátna in the Malá Fatra Mountains.

▶ *Skiing is a popular winter pastime in Slovakia, and the mountains offer a range of slopes suitable for all abilities.*

▼ *There are many historical sites to visit in Slovakia. This is one of the largest castles in Europe, Spišský Hrad.*

Nature

Slovakia might be a small country, but it has plenty of natural beauty. The landscapes can be diverse: high mountain peaks divided by deep valleys and gorges, large forests are broken up by meadows, and green pastures border the fertile lowlands.

▼ *A herd of wild cattle (aurochs) in one of Slovakia's national parks*

Crashing waterfalls in the mountains gradually change into calmly flowing rivers. There are extinct volcanoes, canyons, and caves all over Slovakia, and a wide variety of plants and animals populate this natural setting.

National parks

Many plants and animals in Slovakia are protected, and large areas have been set aside as their habitats. These include national parks, protected landscape areas, and nature reserves, all of which are protected by law. There are more than 1,000 protected territories in Slovakia, covering a total area of almost 4,000 square miles.

There are nine national parks located in and around the Carpathian Mountains. The Tatra National Park is the oldest of its kind in Slovakia. The area was designated as a national park in 1949. It covers the high mountain area of the Tatras and protects the mountain vegetation, such as dwarf pine trees, and other wonderful and rare flora. It also protects the birds and animals that make their homes in the mountains, including eagles, chamois (see box on page 43), marmots (a type of rodent), and lynxes.

▶ *A Slovak shepherd in traditional dress looks over his herd of sheep.*

Chamois, the symbol of the Tatras

The chamois – a species of small antelope that live in the Tatras – are unique, because they developed over the course of 1,000 years in an isolated territory after the glaciers had retreated from this area. The animals differ from their relatives in the Alps and are not found anywhere else on Earth. As there are only about 200 animals remaining, they are strictly protected by law.

The Pieniny National Park is the smallest in Slovakia, but is one of the most beautiful. It is located on the border between Slovakia and Poland. The Dunajec River flows through it, and tourists navigate down the river on rafts so that they can get a better view of the area. In contrast, the national park of Nízké Tatry is the largest and is located in central Slovakia. It is well known for its caves and other limestone landforms.

▼ *The shy chamois live high on the mountain slopes of the Tatra range.*

The national park of Slovensky raj, which is located in the eastern part of the country, was established to protect one of the largest ice caves in the world. It is remarkable for its narrow canyons and deep ravines with waterfalls. Visitors can find their way around the national park using ladders and footbridges.

▼ *Malá Fatra National Park lies in Slovakia's westernmost mountain range.*

The Malá Fatra National Park lies in the westernmost high mountain range of Slovakia. It is known for its extensive dwarf-pine woods, rare plants, and predators such as wolves, lynx, and bears. The national park of Muránska planina, with its wild mountains and limestone landscapes, is still almost untouched by humans.

Poloniny is the easternmost national park in Slovakia. It has extensive oak and fir-oak forests. The name Poloniny comes from its unique high-mountain meadows located below the tree-line (the word means "mountain meadow").

In 2002, two other areas were designated national parks – the national park of Slovensky kras and the national park of Vel'ká Fatra. Slovensky kras is located in the south of Slovakia on the border with Hungary, and is the largest limestone area in Europe. It consists of about 400 caves and gorges. Twelve of them are on the UNESCO list of World Cultural and Natural Heritage. The national park of Vel'ká Fatra, which lies in central Slovakia, is unique because of its well-preserved forests and long valleys. It also contains the highest number of naturally growing yew trees in Europe.

Animals

The fauna or wildlife of Slovakia is varied. More than 40,000 animal species live in its forests. The largest forest inhabitants include bears, wolves, boars, and red deer. The mountain bison is the biggest European land mammal. It lives in western Slovakia in the Topol'čianky nature reserve. Tourists hiking in high mountains are likely to come across chamois or marmots, animals that have adapted well to their harsh surroundings. Predatory birds, such as eagles, goshawks, and falcons also nest in the high mountains.

▲ *The high mountains can be rough territory.*

▼ *In summer, cattle graze in the mountain pastures.*

◀ *A forest with leaf-bearing trees, such as beech, oak, and chestnut*

Many animals live in the fields and meadows. The typical inhabitants of this environment include hares, quails, and partridges, but mice and marmots also make their homes here. The fields of southwestern Slovakia are the habitat of the largest flying European bird, the bustard.

Fish are abundant in streams, lakes, and ponds. Sheatfish, pike, or carp can be caught in the waters of central and northern Slovakia. River otters and many species of waterfowl, such as storks, herons, swans, and ducks live alongside rivers, lakes and streams. The sea eagle, one of the largest predatory birds found in Slovakia, lives along certain parts of the River Danube.

▼ *Many types of fish live in the lakes of Slovakia.*

Forests

In the lowland areas of Slovakia, many of the trees have been cut down, but large forests still exist in the mountains. Compared to other European countries, Slovakia still has a lot of forested areas – amounting to 36 percent of its total surface area. Of all European countries, only Sweden and Austria possess more forest than Slovakia.

The forests are some of Slovakia's greatest natural assets. Continuous broad-leaved, coniferous, or mixed forests cover much of Slovakia. Oak-forests grow in the lowlands and on the lower levels of the mountains because they tend towards a warmer and drier climate.

Away from the mountains in some of the lowland areas, particularly in the towns and settlements, there are protected lime woods. The Slovaks have taken the lime tree as their symbol because of its tenacity and resistance to outside influences. Beech woods, the most frequently occurring type of forest, appear in cooler and rain-prone mountainous areas. This type of forest is also remarkable for the many species of mushrooms that grow there. Slovaks like to gather mushrooms in the autumn and use them in many recipes.

A cold climate, a lot of moisture and less-fertile soil are ideal for spruce trees, which grow at higher altitudes than the beech. They are often mixed with pine or fir trees. Firs are the tallest trees and can reach heights of up to 200 feet. An altitude of nearly 5,000 feet (1,500 meters) is what the experts call the "upper tree line," because no trees grow above it. Instead, there are only dwarf-pine woods and alpine meadows.

Stones cover the highest places in the Tatras and only the most hardy alpine plants such as lichens and mosses grow there. The mountains have bare rock summits. Alluvial forests (plants dependent on water systems to carry and deposit their seeds) composed of willow and poplar trees grow on the river banks. The lower areas are now deforested and are covered instead by fields and meadows.

▼ *Small, isolated lakes can be found among the mountains.*

Environmental issues

The expansion of industry in Slovakia in recent years has resulted in a certain amount of environmental damage, and not enough attention was paid to this by the authorities. Today, however, people realize that nature must be protected and environmental issues addressed. About 22 million tons of waste are produced in Slovakia every year. Each person produces about 750 pounds of household waste a year. Fortunately, there are a number of controlled dumping sites which prevent pollutants seeping into the environment. Environmental protection has become the subject of many legal provisions, although in some cases, they have been adopted too late to save several plant and animal species, which are now extinct.

Waste separation is becoming more common, especially among children. Large housing estates or villages now have a number of containers for different kinds of waste such as paper, glass, plastic bottles, etc. Almost every school organizes collections of waste paper.

Once a month, children go out on the streets to pick up litter. In autumn, they rake up the leaves and clean the area around their schools. Environment and society are subjects taught as part of the school curriculum. Many schools organize events and competitions based on the environment. Children visit animal shelters and help with caring for animals in zoos. They also attend scout clubs where care for the environment is one of the priorities. In many different areas of Slovakia, scouts help to repair haylofts in forests, mark hiking trails, and renovate old mills and wooden structures of historical value. All these efforts will contribute to a better future for Slovakia's natural environment.

What do children think and what can they do?

Romana says, "In our school, classes compete to gather the largest amount of waste paper. Early every Friday morning, a large container is placed in front of the school and children and their parents bring along their waste paper. The teacher, assisted by older boys, weighs the packets of paper and notes down the amount brought by each class. Then the score is displayed on the bulletin board. At the end of the year, the results are announced and prizes are awarded to those who collected the most."

▼ *Most Slovaks realize that they must take care of their environment and preserve the natural beauty of their country.*

Glossary

Constitution A series of laws outlining the basic principles of a government or country.

Gothic An ornate style of architecture dating from the Middle Ages.

Habsburg Empire The land under control of the German royal family, who gained the thrones of several countries, including Austria and Hungary, from the late Middle Ages to the twentieth century.

Megalith A type of construction using large stones.

Middle Ages The period from around AD 500 to 1450.

Neanderthals Early people, usually associated with Stone Age cultures.

Orthodox Church The Christian Church in the East; it has several independent sects, including Greek and Russian Orthodox.

Reformation The rise of Protestantism in Europe in the sixteenth century.

Slavs A large group of European people with similar languages. Individual tribes descended from the Slavs include Slovaks, Czechs, Poles, Serbs and Croats.

Stone Age The earliest period in technological history, when tools and weapons were made from stone.

Tartars A group of Mongolian tribes who invaded Europe in the thirteenth century.

Index

Websites

www.lonelyplanet.com/destinations/europe/slovakia
www.cia.gov/cia/publications/factbook/geos/lo.html
www.dfat.gov.au/geo/slovakia
www.slovakia.org